All the animals in Mr Ringmaster's circus laugh when the storks bring Mrs Jumbo a baby. Whoever heard of an elephant with huge pink ears? But when little Dumbo meets Timothy Mouse, he discovers something that just might make him the star of the show...

British Library Cataloguing in Publication Data
Walt Disney's Dumbo.
  813'.52[J]   PZ7
  ISBN 0-7214-1035-9

First edition

Published by Ladybird Books Ltd Loughborough Leicestershire UK
Ladybird Books Inc Auburn Maine 04210 USA

Printed in England (7)

Disney

DUMBO

Ladybird Books

The animals in Mr Ringmaster's
circus were all very excited. For
during the night the storks had
come visiting, bringing babies to
some of the mothers in the circus.

4

Baby Giraffe had come first,
followed by a giggly Baby
Kangaroo and a hairy Baby Bear.

But there was no Baby Elephant.

Mrs Jumbo tried hard not to cry. The storks had brought her nothing, and they would not be back for another year.

No one noticed how sad she was,
for everyone was bustling about
and getting ready for a journey.

Mr Ringmaster's circus was moving
on to another town, and they all
had a train to catch.

7

As the circus train began to pull away, a stork, wearing a postman's hat, suddenly appeared high above.

"Special delivery! Special delivery!" he screamed. His wings flapped wildly as he puffed and panted to keep up with the train.

In his beak, the stork was carrying a bundle. "Mrs Jumbo!" he cried. "It's for you!" He let go of the bundle, and Mrs Jumbo stretched out her trunk to catch it safely.

Mrs Jumbo wondered what was inside. Carefully she untied the bundle. And there it was! A baby elephant!

"How beautiful he is," she said, cuddling him with her trunk.

All the elephants crowded round
and came to look at the new
arrival. "Isn't he sweet!" they
said.

But when they looked more closely,
they fell silent. Then they began to
giggle. And then they began to
laugh.

"Look at his ears!" called one of them. For instead of neat little elephant ears, Mrs Jumbo's new baby had enormous pink ears.

Mrs Jumbo glared at the elephants, and sent them away. "I'm going to call you *Dumbo*," she murmured. The baby elephant waggled his ears, settled himself into a comfortable position and fell fast asleep.

Next morning, the train stopped
and all the animals climbed out.
The circus men put up a big tent
and the animals lined up in a
procession, with Mrs Jumbo and
Dumbo at the back. "This is called
the *parade*," she told Dumbo.

"Just follow me."

But Dumbo kept falling over his big ears. The people watching the parade laughed at him and poor Dumbo began to cry.

After the parade some naughty boys came up and began teasing Dumbo. Mrs Jumbo picked up the leader and gave him a good hard smack with her trunk.

She had only wanted to teach the boy a lesson for being cruel, but the people thought she had gone mad. They began to scream and run to safety. The circus men came running with ropes. "We'll have to lock her up," shouted one of them.

And Dumbo watched in tears as his mother was dragged away.

Poor Dumbo didn't understand.
No one took any notice of him
and, tired and frightened, he crept
back to the elephant tent.

But the elephants had decided that
Mrs Jumbo had brought disgrace
to their good name. They wanted

nothing to do with Dumbo and wouldn't even speak to him.

So that night Dumbo lay down and cried himself to sleep.

Dumbo woke up suddenly.
Someone was tickling him!

There, standing in front of him,
was a furry little creature wearing a
smart red coat and a cap with a
feather in it.

"I saw everything that happened,"
he whispered. "I'm going to help
you. But first," he added, "I'm
going to put the fear of mouse into
those stuck-up elephants!"

The mouse tiptoed towards the
elephants. He stood behind them
and **ROARED!**

The elephants went pale. "Eek!"
they screamed. "Eek! It's a
mouse! Eek!"

The mouse stood in the middle of
the tent, roaring away. The
elephants fled in terror.

The mouse grinned at Dumbo.
"I'm Timothy Mouse," he said.
"I may be small, but I can cause
big trouble. And now," he said,
adjusting his hat, "we're going to
set your mother free."

Dumbo told Timothy about how
the people laughed at him.

Timothy examined the elephant's
ears. "Hmmm!" he said, putting
his head on one side to think.

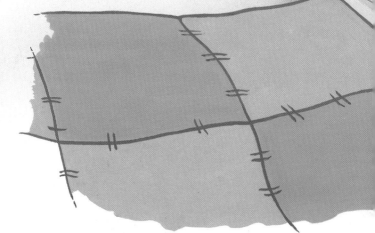

At last he snapped his fingers.
"I've got it!" he said. "We'll
make you into a star! Then they'll
do anything for you."

So that night, when Mr Ringmaster
lay sound asleep, Timothy crept up
and whispered into his ear,

"Your circus needs a star jumbo,
Your star should be my friend, Dumbo!"

Mr Ringmaster woke up the next morning, full of a marvellous idea he had had during the night: Dumbo was going to be his new star!

So he ordered the elephants to make a huge elephant pyramid! Then Dumbo was to jump off a high trapeze and land on top of them all!

It all went well in the rehearsal but,
during the show, nothing went
right. Dumbo knocked the
elephants over, and they all came
crashing down in a heap.

Mr Ringmaster was angry, and he
sent Dumbo to bed without any
supper.

"You are no good at being a star,"
said Mr Ringmaster, the next day,
"but you *can* make people laugh.
Go and work with the clowns!"

Dumbo hated his new job. He was scared when the clowns made him jump through some flames down into a tub of water.

But the people watching the show thought it was very funny and the clowns decided to keep Dumbo in their act.

Dumbo was very sad. So that night, when everyone else was fast asleep, Timothy Mouse took Dumbo to see his mother.

Dumbo put his trunk through the window, and gave a soft whimper. Mrs Jumbo was so pleased to see him, and she cuddled him with her long trunk until it was time to say goodnight.

"Goodbye!" she whispered. "Be good." And Dumbo went back to the circus.

Now the clowns had opened a
bottle of bubbly champagne to
celebrate their success. Some of it
had spilled into a water barrel
outside their tent.

On the way home Timothy and
Dumbo were thirsty, so the two
friends stopped to have a drink
from the water barrel.

Afterwards they began to feel quite
giddy. They began to run and jump
and dance. And then, quite
suddenly, they felt tired, and fell
sound asleep.

Dumbo woke up next morning and realised that he and Timothy had been sleeping at the very top of a high tree!

Some crows, who were perching in a tree, thought it was all very funny.

"How did you get to the top of the tree?" asked one of the crows.

Dumbo thought and thought. Then he remembered that he had dreamt that he was flying through the air with Timothy tucked inside his yellow cap.

"Perhaps you weren't dreaming!" said Timothy excitedly. "Perhaps you really *were* flying!" He gave Dumbo a feather. "Try to fly!" he said. "You can if you hold onto this magic feather!"

Dumbo stood on the edge of a cliff and looked down. The crows gave him a push, and suddenly he was flying!

Timothy and the crows
cheered. For they knew
that the feather wasn't
really magic. It was just an
ordinary feather. Dumbo
could really and truly fly!

For their evening performance, the clowns were going to catch Dumbo on a little trampoline. He had to jump from the top of the tent but he wasn't frightened any longer. He had his magic feather, and he was going to *fly* down to the ground.

Just at the right moment he jumped. But to his horror he dropped the feather! It floated away, and Dumbo began to plunge towards the ground far below.

As Dumbo fell, he heard Timothy's voice shouting to him, "Fly, Dumbo! It isn't a magic feather! You *can* fly!"

And Dumbo started to flap his ears as though they were wings. Soon he was swooping up, up, up to the top of the tent.

The crowd gasped in amazement.
They had never seen anything so
wonderful!

Dumbo was the new star of the
circus, just as Timothy had
promised!

Soon crowds were flocking to
Mr Ringmaster's circus to see the
flying elephant.

Mr Ringmaster was delighted and
Mrs Jumbo was set free! From
then on, the two elephants were

given their own comfortable
carriage to travel in, all to
themselves.

Well, not quite to themselves. For,
tucked comfortably inside Dumbo's
cap, was Timothy Mouse. After
all, he was Dumbo's best friend!